£4.99
UK Only

Gladiators Fan Club

If you would like to join the official Gladiators Fan Club, write for details to:
PO Box 158
Sevenoaks Kent
TN15 8GF

™ © LWTP 1992/93/94/95
Made in association with the Samuel Goldwyn Company.
All rights reserved.
Published in Great Britain by World International, an imprint of Egmont Publishing Ltd., Egmont House, PO Box 111, Great Ducie Street, Manchester M60 3BL.
Printed in the UK.
ISBN 0-7498-2395-X

Written by Alison Daniels, Martin Steale
Produced by Newsstand Services
Edited by Alan Young
Designed by John Derbyshire

Note – Play Safely

Gladiators and contenders have undergo considerable training – do NOT attempt to imita their actions or recreate Gladiator even

CONTENTS

6.	LET BATTLE COMMENCE!
8.	WOLF
10.	JET
12.	TROJAN
14.	LIGHTNING
16.	CELEBRITY GLADIATORS
18.	THE EVENTS
24.	SARACEN
26.	ZODIAC
28.	HUNTER
30.	AMAZON
32.	INTERNATIONAL GLADIATORS
36.	RHINO
38.	COBRA
40.	NIGHTSHADE
42.	WARRIOR
44.	VOGUE
46.	YOUR QUESTIONS ANSWERED
48.	COMPETITION WINNERS – LAST YEAR'S WINNERS
50.	PANTHER
52.	RAIDER
54.	FALCON
56.	JOHN & ULRIKA'S MAGIC MOMENTS
58.	THE WINNERS
60.	GLADIATORS COMPETITION!

Welcome to the 1996 Gladiators Annual, packed with great new pictures and interviews with all your favourite Gladiators.

The programme has certainly seen some changes over the last year but one thing hasn't changed - all the Gladiators and contenders make sure they do the very best they can, and they never disappoint!

The response to last year's annual was staggering - so staggering in fact that we took some of the questions you've been asking and put them to the Gladiators themselves. You'll find the answers on page 46.

There were thousands of entries to the Gladiators competition last year, and we hope it will be the same this time round. The winners are on page 48 and there's a all-new competition on page 60. You coul win a bicycle, a selection of Gladiators games or a great Wolf T-shirt. Good luck!

In the meantime and in between time - k watching Gladiators, keep facing the Ultimate Challenge, but above all, keep sa Play on!

GLADIATORS 6

PLAY ON!

GLADIATORS 7

IN PROFILE...

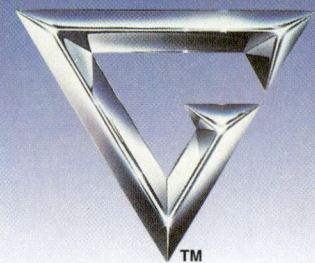

..a villain, and he loves his work

WOLF

DID YOU KNOW?
Wolf owns his own gym and when he's busy, it is not unusual for him to open it up at 2 o'clock in the morning in order to complete his daily training routine!

Wolf has been expanding on his acting career this y[ear] appearing in two films, entitled *The Bruce* and *So[ul] Stealers*. In both movies, he plays - guess what? - a villain, a[nd] he loves his work! "Hopefully, I can be the next Christopher L[ee] or Donald Pleasance or Peter Cushing," he says. "There's a niche there and I'd like to fill it."

But this popular Gladiator has also been busy doing his fair share of PA's and says he is astonished - and delighted - to [find] that people will travel miles to see him when they know he i[s] making an appearance. So what is the appeal of this bad guy[?]

"I think basically it keeps people on the edge of their seats," [he] says. "When I come out, they don't know what's going to happen. And I'm basically their crusader, as well as being a baddie. If a contender is being very arrogant or cocky, they'll say, 'Wait till he meets Wolf!', and they can't wait for me to clash with them. Also, I think anyone who flouts the rules or bends them a little always adds a bit more excitement to the show. If everyone came out and was really nice, it wouldn't b[e] as exciting as having someone to boo and hiss at!"

And it doesn't sound as if Wolf is ready to mend his ways in [the] new series of Gladiators. "They first introduced the red card [at] the live shows in Sheffield, and I kept getting it!" he snarls.

The way this Gladiator carries on, he'll soon be collecting the whole pack!

STATISTICS
Date of Birth:
    30th September 1952
Home: Sevenoaks, Kent
Height: 6'
Weight: 15 stone
Chest: 48"
Waist: 30"
Bicep: 18"

IN PROFILE...

Jet is generally thought to be the sweetest, smiliest Gladiator - but, as she explains, she can also be fiercely competitive when she steps into the arena!

"When that button is pressed - boy, watch out!" she laughs. " keep it well in check, because it can be a very negative, jeal destructive emotion, but like any actress, I will pick on it whe need to, and when John (Anderson, referee) blows his whistl BAM, I'm there! But when he blows the whistle at the end of the event, I switch it off again."

Contenders in the new series had better beware, because thi year, Jet has employed a new coach and has been working c maximising her potential as an athlete. "To get to where I am a Glad, I've had the natural talent from being a gymnast and dancer," she observes, "but I'd like to see how good a Gladia I can be after being trained like an athlete, like our contende

"My absolute strengths are agility, mobility and flexibility, bu need to concentrate on my strength and short burst stamina endurance, as well as the sports-specific stuff like climbing."

Hill running forms an important part of Jet's exercise programme and during that part of her work-out, you'll alway find her dog, Ben, at her side. A border collie/German shephe cross, Jet picked him out at a Canine Defence League shelter last year. "He's so loving and so special, he really is," she enthuses. "He's my No. 1 training partner!"

JET
.....agility, mobility and flexibility

DID YOU KNOW?
Jet plans to embark on an Open University degree in science.

GLADIATORS 10

STATISTICS
Date of Birth: 13th February 1970
Home: Surrey
Height: 5'7"
Weight: 9 stone, 8lbs
Chest: 38"
Waist: 25"

IN PROFILE...

TROJAN

"I chase 'em, catch 'em and run 'em down!"

DID YOU KNOW?
Trojan owns a valuable collection of cartoon film cells and is looking to add to it all the time.

Trojan is one Gladiator who always seems to be on the g When he has some spare time, he loves to write and ha already had a film screenplay considered by a Hollywood film producer, as well as penning a book entitled *Seeing Is Believing*, about his life as a Gladiator, for which he hopes to find a publish Plus, he is also involved in a TV production company, from which hopes to learn more about what goes on behind the scenes.

But naturally, keeping himself in peak condition as a Gladiator is main priority and at 8.30 in the morning, you're likely to find him soaked in sweat as he works out on an exercise bike during the of the two training sessions that he undertakes every day. When leads such a busy life, when does he find time to sleep?!

"I try to go for 40 minutes a night," he quips, before admitting m seriously, "no, I always get eight to ten hours. I cram everything but I'm very relaxed; I've got too many important things to think about to waste time being edgy. I'm very laid-back and my philosophy is: If it's going to happen, it'll happen."

Viewers of the the most recent series of Gladiators were treated a slightly slimmed-down Trojan, as he managed to drop his weigh down to 15 stone, so that he could be more agile when taking pa in the Ultimate Challenge.

"Nowadays, the events are gearing more towards pursuit-type of things," he explains. "And I think it's for the best - the more chas the more excitment - so I want to be fitter and faster. I like to le the contenders take a couple of steps and then I chase 'em, catc 'em and run 'em down!"

STATISTICS

Date of Birth: 25th February 1968
Home: Central London
Height: 6'2"
Weight: 15 stone
Chest: 50"
Waist: 34"
Bicep: 20"

IN PROFILE...

LIGHTNING

Aggressive and hard hitting

DID YOU KNOW?
Lightning first started training as a gymnast at the age of six, but often had to sit out of the class for ten minutes, because she used to get fits of giggles!

Lightning has been one busy lady this year. Not only does she have a hectic schedule in her work as a Gladiator, but she's also appeared in pantomime, moved hous[e], decorated her new home and planned her September weddin[g] in Sri Lanka! In between all this activity, she's also had to fit her workout routine, but she's solved that problem by kitting her garage with fitness equipment, such as dumbbells, a stai[r] climber and a bicycle, and turning it into a gym!

"With my work schedule, you can't always fit in going to the gym at a certain time," she says. "But whatever time it is, ev[en] if it's ten o'clock at night, I can just nip out to the garage!"

With all the running around that she's been doing this year, Lightning has also found that she's accidentally lost a few pounds, but she's determined to regain them in time for the new series. "I'm concentrating on getting a bit more beefy, because throughout the live shows (at Sheffield last Easter), although I was still as aggressive and hitting as hard, becaus[e I] didn't have the body weight, I found that I was getting aches and pains," she says. "So I shall eat more carbohydrates and protein and train more heavily to get a little more weight beh[ind] me."

Lightning had her most successful series so far last year and hopes to keep improving. "I think the first couple of years, I w[as] a bit nervous, but I just put my mind to it last time and now [I] hope I'll keep it going this year," she says. "There's no reason why I shouldn't, really, as long as I keep my fitness and my s[trength]. I'm looking forward to it!"

STATISTICS
Date of Birth: 25th December 1971
Home: Oxfordshire
Height: 5' 7"
Weight: 9 stone 8 lbs.
Chest: 39"
Waist: 25"

GLADIATORS 15

CELEBRITY GLADIATORS

Last year's Celebrity Gladiators turned out to be packed with thrills and excitement as some of sport's top stars turned out to pit themselves against the Ultimate Challenge!

Eddie Kidd (motorcycling)

Martin Offiah (rugby)

THE EVENTS
What The Gladiators Say

ELIMINATOR

All the Gladiators agree that this is the hardest event. Of course, none of them will ever take part in it, because this is strictly contender territory. It's the make or break event which forms the climax of any Gladiators show, as two contenders, pushed to the very limit of their endurance, struggle to make it over this most demanding of obstacle courses. The contender with the highest number of points from previous events gets a head start, receiving a half second for each point they are ahead.

The contenders must tackle four over-and-under beams, a rope climb, a stamina-sapping hand-bike over 20ft for the men, and a overhead ladder for the women. Then there's the tricky 20ft rolling beam followed by the cargo net onto the high platform. From there it's the zip line, which drops them 90 feet back to earth and on to the hardest part of all - the Travelator. Once they struggle to the top it's just a quick rope swing to victory!

Nightshade doesn't like to feel that there is any event on Gladiators that she can't be very good at. "I've always wanted to get a time over the Eliminator, she says. "I've gone over it in practice but of course I'm not allowed to do it in the show."

POLE-AXE

This vertical sprint requires speed, strength, stamina, skill - and nerves of steel. It's a one-on-one race to the top of that glistening 40ft pole by way of the rungs set into the side. Climbing them mea that contenders and Gladiators alike must circumnavigate the pole usually in less than ten seconds! The first to the summit then has chance to "pole-axe" their opponent by slamming a button which v retract their rungs, casting them down to the 6ft-high mats below. Contenders receive 10 points should they succeed.

The undisputed master is Hunter, who makes it all look so easy. "It's all about rhythm. Like when you're doing hurdles you get yourself into a rhythm and it's so many steps here, then jump, so many steps here, then jump. It's exactly the same with Pole-Axe. You count the pegs so you know how f you've got to go and I would just bang the button when I reached the top, I wouldn't need to look up because I'd kno exactly where I was."

PURSUIT

s tough assault course is all about speed and agility and the
ale Gladiators tend to be more successful on this event than their
e counterparts. Contenders get a three second start and must
erse a tricky balancing plank, overhead ladder, wobbly wire,
stic netting and a rope climb. The winner gets 10 points, the
ner-up 5, with no points awarded to anyone who gets caught by
ladiator.

one of Nightshade's favourites. "I enjoy Pursuit, it's
ood game. I like it because it's very similar to the
minator, which we're not allowed to do in the show.
suit is the only chance Gladiators get to take part
an Eliminator-type event."

nther adds, "The audience like the idea of Gladiators
ng the Eliminator, I think that's why Pursuit was
ented. But ultimately I think the Gladiators would
her do the Eliminator."

PYRAMID

Contenders have just one action-packed minute to scale this giant 25ft pyramid comprised of 2ft steps. It would be simple if it weren't for the Gladiators descending on them from the top. Contenders are at a disadvantage and many of them try to take out their Gladiator so they can rush to the top unhindered. But this is easier said than done.

Jet is a great lover of this event and found her gymnastic skill and natural speed a great help. "Pyramid is my favourite game without a doubt. I really enjoy it. It's harder for the contender, because they have to get all the way up, which is very tiring, but we only have to come down and stop them. Agility and all-round fitness helped me with that. I'm not really a heavy, but I proved myself to be tougher than a lot of people thought in that event."

HIT & RUN

can run, but you can't hide from the Hit & Run balls hurled by
diators as contenders try to negotiate the 24ft rope bridge. Each
e they get across the bridge, which is suspended 12 feet above
ground, the contenders earn themselves 2 points, but four
diators are ever ready to send them flying with one swing of their
hty demolition balls.

diators who have been injured in competition often enjoy this
nt because it gives them a chance to compete, even if they're not
e up to taking part in full-contact events like Powerball or
amid.

not one of Panther's favourites, as she prefers to get
ysical with the contenders. "Personally I find it a bit
ing," she says, "because you're just standing there
nging this ball and if the person doesn't come off then
a non-event in my eyes. A lot of people seem to
 it, though."

GLADIATORS 19

ATLASPHERES

The giant 7ft diameter balls of Atlaspheres cut a mighty spectacle as they career around the arena. Both contenders have 60 seconds to avoid two Gladiators who are doing their utmost to stop them making contact with the four pods dotted around the playing area.

To make things more exciting, the contenders are not allowed to score on the pod nearest to them when they first enter the arena - not until they have attempted to score at another pod or made contact with a Gladiator. Gladiators are not allowed to double-team their opponents and are not allowed to detain a contender for more than ten seconds.

Trojan says, "Although it looks easy, Atlaspheres is quite hard, but it's a nice game."

Warrior adds, "You have to be very aerobically fit to do Atlaspheres, because you have to be very explosive for a minute. Really, it's the contender who should be doing all the work, because you control the middle of the arena, if you do it right. I try never to chase the contender; I try to cut him off and block him in a corner, and I've never had that many pods scored against me."

TILT

This event is heavily weighted in the contender's favour, since it is easier to pull someone down than to pull them up. The Gladiator is always on the higher table, which is angled forwards, the contender on the lower table which is angled back. But the Gladiators tend to hold their own in this event because of their superior body weight.

The event lasts just 30 seconds but the looks of effort on the faces of those taking part show that it's no picnic. The contender has two chances to pull the Gladiator off his platform, and gets 5 points each time he or she succeeds.

Panther, who was injured when she fell off her platform during this event, still says she enjoys it. "The secret is to get into a position where you can tip your platform back. Once you do that you shouldn't come off."

But it's not one of Trojan's favourites. "I despise that game! It's geared so much towards the contenders and the angle of the board is very hard. It's horrible when you look down. I hate it!"

Warrior thinks differently, "It's a good game for me, because of my body weight, but the bias is towards the contender on that game, make no mistake about that! I think all the other guys have been pulled off, but touch wood, I haven't yet!"

DANGER ZONE

A tough event for the contenders, but a relatively easy one for the Gladiators. From their platform at the end of the arena, the Gladiator's task is to use their tennis ball launcher to hit the contender, who at the same time is trying desperately to hit a target above the Gladiator with the aid of similar tennis ball launchers strategically placed at different safety stations around the arena.

But the safety stations are programmed to auto-destruct at ten second intervals unless the contender reaches them. So they only have a few seconds to aim, fire and then run to the next station, while all the time a vigilant Gladiator is watching their every move, knowing they will soon have to make a break for it across the arena floor or be disqualified. For a hit to register, it must be direct, ricochets do not count. Contenders receive 1 point for each station achieved, 10 points if they hit the target above the Gladiator, or 5 points if they hit the secondary target below the Gladiator.

Cobra says, "I like Danger Zone because it's easy to do and it's great fun to shoot at the contenders."

JOUST

...ther event that many Gladiators find difficult. "The thing is, you ...'t get a really good whack in," says Hunter. "You want to get ...e serious power behind your blows but when you're moving about ... that you just can't and that tends to be frustrating."

...ride their violently bucking sky bikes, Gladiators and contenders ...e one minute to unseat each other with the help ...heir combat club. This event is so difficult that ...tenders get five points just for staying on! If ... unseat a Gladiator, or if the Gladiator falls, ... get 10 points. If they lose their combat club, ...ever, they get no points.

...an says, "I'm currently unbeaten on this ... and I broke two pugil sticks while ...mpeting at this year's live show in ...ffield! The important thing in this event is ...hold the stick with both hands and hit as ...d as you can!"

GAUNTLET

... is perhaps the ultimate test of a contender's guts in the face of ... one, but five Gladiators, each and every one determined to stop ...m in their tracks.

... Gauntlet is 45 metres long and the contender has 30 seconds to ...e it past each of the defenders, whose mission is to slow him or ... down using their ram rods. If the run is completed in under 20 ...nds, a maximum 10 points can be won. If they make it in under ...seconds there are 5 points on offer. There are no points for effort ...ey fail to complete the course.

... Gladiators' task is made more difficult by the fact that they are ...allowed to hold the contender down, or deliberately push them ... of bounds.

...ther says, "Gauntlet's a good rough and tumble event and ... a good chance to see a few Gladiators working together."

HANG TOUGH

This exciting game of aerial chess is acted out over a playing area measuring 50ft by 25ft. A series of rings dangles from the ceiling, ten feet above the ground and about four feet apart. The contender has 60 seconds in which he or she can either 'hang tough' in the scoring area in the centre of the arena, or go for broke and try to make it all the way across to the platform opposite. They are not allowed to remain on the same ring for more than ten seconds.

The Gladiator can pull the contender off by tugging at them or prying their fingers off the rings. No headlocks or hitting is allowed and John Anderson has previously warned Wolf for raising his legs too high when he's trying to get a grip on his opponent.

If the contender makes it across the arena, he or she will receive 10 points, if they are in the scoring area when the referee calls time up, they will receive 5 points.

Lightning is the undisputed queen of this event. Her upper body strength and her unparalleled ability to traverse between the rings gives her a great advantage in the air. She says, "I love the feeling of swinging around on the rings - it's fantastic! You're not using your speed or your power - it's more elegant than that and you concentrate on the flow. Traversing is also very important, because if you keep going in the same direction you'll go straight into the fly trap!"

DUEL

This event comes right out of the Gladiator tradition of old: one to one combat with no quarter asked for nor given. Both contender and Gladiator are evenly matched on identical platforms, ten feet off the ground, four feet in diameter and 16 inches apart. Duel requires total concentration and a lot of nerve. It can often turn into a battle of wills, as one tries to unnerve the other and force them into making a mistake.

The rules state that if a contender or a Gladiator is knocked down to a kneeling or sitting position on the platform, they must attempt to return to a standing position immediately or face disqualification. The same goes if either of them crosses between the two platforms while the contest is on or if they lose their pugil stick. 10 points are granted for a win, 5 points for a draw.

Trojan says, "I have a saying for this one. 'Once a pupil, now a master, you face me, you face disaster!' I go for head shots on this one and bash as hard as I can!"

SUSPENSION BRIDGE

Gladiators meets Indiana Jones for this one-to-one battle o strength and skill. Contender and Gladiator advance on eac other along the swinging rope bridge, each wielding their hammer head with which they must attempt to knock eac other off. They aren't allowed to push - a direct hit must b landed to dispose of their opponent. If contender or Gladia are knocked to their knees they have five seconds to get u or risk disqualification. 10 points are awarded if the conten dispatches the Gladiator from the bridge (provided they sta on themselves). 5 points are on offer in the case of a draw

Zodiac says, "A lot of it is luck and balance, but you also got to be extremely aggressive. It's not my favourite game. I'm one of the lightest Gladiators and a lot of the tim the female contenders are heavier th I am, and obviously, that's a big fact because it really is body weight vers body weight."

THE WALL

The 36ft high Wall is one of the most daunting events in the Gladiatorial arena It's tricky enough to find handholds on t surface, but the knowledge that a determined Gladiator is on your tail is enough to throw some contenders into a panic as they try to scale their way to th rafters of Birmingham's National Indoor Arena.

Even so, a ten second start means that most contenders are able to escape the clutches of their pursuer and make it to the top. The Gladiator's task is not just to reach the contender, but to physically p him or her clear of the Wall itself. Once they have caught their prey, t Gladiator may jump free of the Wall, provided they keep hold of their designated contender. As in all other events, contenders may struggle with their pursuers but kicking is strictly forbidden, and punishable by disqualification.

This is another one of Jet's favourites. The suppleness of her body and her natural speed are superb allies for this gruelling event. "You've got to stay focused," she says. "You can't just blaze up the Wall, you've got to concentrate on what you're doing. A lot of people just panic because they're reaching for everything and not concentrating properly on what they're doi

SWINGSHOT

...is visually one of the most exciting events, with ...participants swinging every which way in their ...st for the coloured balls which mean more ...ts, and more precious seconds won for the ...minator.

...tenders and Gladiators begin the event on ...arate platforms raised about 15 feet from the ...und. They must jump first to the floor, then up ...he pole suspended from the ceiling, on which ...balls are stuck. Yellow balls are worth 1 point, ...are worth 2 and red 3 points. The Gladiators' ...is to obstruct, distract and generally disrupt ...contenders' chances of scoring. They can make ...attempt to stop contenders getting the balls except for blows to ...head or kicking. Nor are they allowed to deliberately remove the ...s from the pole.

...tenders must return the balls to the container on their platform ...the points to be counted. If, however, they hesitate on the ...form for more than three seconds before returning to play, they ...forfeit their last score. The event lasts one minute.

...con says, "The technique with Swingshot is knowing where to hit the ground precisely to get that big rebound off the jump. You're also keeping your eye on the contender the whole time and trying to anticipate when they're going to jump. You have to leave your platform a split second before they do, so that you have the time to get there in front of them."

POWER-BALL

This rugby-style contest is a favourite with many of the Gladiators, who enjoy the opportunity to put their strength and weight to good use. Contenders have one minute to place as many of their balls in the five containers as possible. Stopping them are three Gladiators who may block, push or tackle to prevent the contenders reaching their goal. Any combination of Gladiators is allowed to deter the contenders, but they must release their victim if they have been held down for more than three seconds.

Contenders must return to the opposite bucket from which they picked up their last ball. A score in one of the four outer containers gets 2 points, a score in the centre bucket wins 4 points.

Hunter says, "Powerball is very much a tactical game. People often don't realise it, but we have very specific tactics in that game. If you've got the tactics right, you know exactly where the other men are going to be. I tend to run the middle in Powerball, which means I'm watching both ends, so I've got to be on the ball, otherwise I get my wrists slapped by the two end guys!"

Wolf says, "I love Powerball, but there has to be a lot of co-ordination with whoever's playing in the middle, because sometimes you're faced by two chaps and you have to guard one particular pod and you just have to pray that somebody is guarding the others. It's a very tough game and there's a lot of things you can and can't do. I've been told off quite a few times for pushing people out of the arena completely."

SKYTRAK

This topsy-turvy game has everyone in the audience on the edge of their seats, craning their necks to catch the action unfolding on the ceiling. Contenders get a five second head start before the Gladiators set off in pursuit. Expert hand and foot co-ordination is required to manage the hairpin bends of the figure-of-eight track as all four race to the finish. If a Gladiator reaches the detonator being pulled behind the contender it will explode in a shower of sparks, making this one of the most spectacular events in the arena. The first contender home receives 10 points, the second 5 points. No points are awarded if they are caught by a Gladiator.

Saracen says, "The main thing with Skytrak is to watch your knees, especially when you spin off like a racing car, it's very easy to hurt them! It's a difficult event to do well because you're upside down and you can easily get disorientated, but there's no special trick to it - you just go like the clappers!"

GLADIATORS 23

IN PROFILE...

...Coming back with a vengeance...

SARACEN

DID YOU KNOW?
Saracen is the only Gladiator with a full-time day job. In real life, he is a fireman.

Saracen is already looking forward to the next series Gladiators, because he believes the programme improves and becomes more exciting with each successive y

"The show has become better, because now there is more variety in the events," he explains. "In the first series, we onl had six events, so it was the same every week, whereas now we have more, with different events in every programme. Th best part of it is, we don't know what games we're going to put on and neither do the contenders, so you have to be goo at every single event.

"There were only two games I missed out last year. I retired myself from the Wall, because I was suffering badly from tendonitis - and I didn't do the Joust in the last series. Otherwise, I'm a jack of all trades!"

Saracen injured his knee at the live shows at Sheffield Arena while he was taking part in Powerball, and had to use a concentrated programme of exercises to strengthen it up aga in time for this year's shows.

And he has a serious message for would-be contenders: "Saracen's going to be back next year - stronger, probably bigger, faster, tougher and he's going to be angrier than he's ever been before! So beware - Saracen is coming back with vengeance!"

STATISTICS

Date of Birth: 30th August 1963
Home: London
Height: 6' 3"
Weight: 17 and a half stone
Chest: 54"
Waist: 32"
Bicep: 20"

IN PROFILE...

As a pole vauter in the British athletics team, out of all the Gladiators, Zodiac is probably the one who trains most intensively all the year round. Before filming a new series of Gladiators or taking part in a major athletics event, she embarks on a 12-week training programme.

"The first six weeks, I do quite a lot of endurance to work to build up my stamina and that consists of maybe two or three mile distances and heavy weights, and then the last six weeks get down to explosive work and lots and lots of reps on the weights."

To keep her interest level high, she generally trains with a group of fellow pole vaulters, so that they can all give each other encouragement and moral support. "It does help, especially if you're training at quite a high intensity," she explains. "There are days when you feel fed up and don't want to go to do two or three hours at the gym, and it helps if you've got other people around you."

She also finds that a sense of team spirit is also a major motivation when she competes in the arena during the Gladiators series. "Last year, all the female Gladiators would huddle together backstage or warm up together before actually going out, and each time, a different girl would say, 'Right, come on - we're Gladiators, we're here for a reason, let's go and do the business!'" she remembers. "Having people behind you makes all the difference!"

ZODIAC

DID YOU KNOW?

Zodiac is a champion pole vaulter, who improved on the sport's Commonwealth record three times during an indoor event featuring Russia against Great Britain earlier this year and is now ranked eighth in the world.

Training intensively all year round

STATISTICS

Date of Birth: 2nd November 1965
Home: Woking, Surrey
Height: 5' 9"
Weight: 9 stone 10 lbs
Chest: 36"
Waist: 24"

GLADIATORS 27

IN PROFILE...

The serious ice cream eater...
HUNTER

DID YOU KNOW?
As well as being a Gladiator, Hunter also has a successful modelling career and is currently featured in the catalogue of a fashion company that specialises in clothing for larger men.

Hunter owes his muscular physique to his experience a bodybuilder, but now that he's a Gladiator, while still keeping himself toned and in good shape, he's lost some weig to make him more nimble and agile when he's undertaking th events. As well as his bodybuilding training, his exercise regim these days also incorporates a lot of fat-burning work, which includes five to ten mile runs in the countryside around his h in York.

However, about eight weeks before the new series of Gladiato begins, he will modify his schedule to involve activities that a specifically geared towards the events featured in the programme. "For Duel, I do a lot of boxing, because it's the s technique - explosive power for 30 seconds to a minute," he explains. "I'll do a lot of hill running to practise for Pyramid a I'll do climbing, which is a hobby of mine anyway, to help on Wall."

However, he is very aware that over-training can result in burn-out and so this good-looking Gladiator also makes sure that he puts some time aside for rest and relaxation.

"As my whole life is based around sport, when I do have any time off, I like to go out and meet my friends for a drink or a meal in a restaurant, go for a steam or a sauna if my body's sore, or just stay at home and watch TV," he says.

"And one day a week, I forget my diet and eat what I like. I t to go to the cinema every Sunday and eat *serious* ice cream! don't care what film I see, as long as I've got my ice cream!"

STATISTICS

Date of Birth:
          12th June 1973
Home: York
Height: 6'3"
Weight: 16 stone 10 lbs
Chest: 50"
Waist: 34"
Bicep: 18"

IN PROFILE...

AMAZON

became Gladiator almost by accident

New Gladiator, Amazon, has actually been involved in the TV programme for some time. Before she became a Gladiator she was an Olympic swimmer and co-presented the first *Train To Win* show for junior Gladiators. She is married to Gladiators coach, Derek Redmond - but she became a Gladiator almost by accident! When auditions were being held for new Gladiators earlier this year, she went along merely to help Derek out, but the producers were so impressed by her fitness as she did demonstrations for hopeful applicants that they asked her if she would join the team herself.

Since joining the Gladiators, Amazon says that she has not had to adapt her usual training routine too much. "My fitness and my strength levels are fine, because I work out every day," she explains. "I'm used to being an Olympic athlete and I'm used to training. Some days it's cardiovascular work and others, it's weight work. What I have done is probably upped my weight work to try to increase a little bit of strength.

"But what I've had to learn which is very specific to Gladiators is how to tackle, to climb and to take a knock. Particularly climbing, because with Gladiators, forearm strength is very important, because you have to hold on to so many things, whether it's a contender or a pugil stick!"

DID YOU KNOW?
Initially, Amazon and the Gladiators' producers tried to think of a Gladiators name that related to water or swimming, to tie in with her sporting past. But they couldn't think of anything suitable, so she was named Amazon, after the warrior women of Greek mythology, because she's so tall!

STATISTICS
Date of Birth:
　　　　　1st November 1962
Home: 　　Northampton
Height: 　 5' 11"
Weight: 　10 and a half stone
Chest: 　　38"
Waist: 　　26"

GLADS

They came from the ends of the earth to do battle in the arena. Men and women of colossal strength, extreme courage and matchless skill travelled Britain to demonstrate the heights they had reached through their training and talent and dedication. The British Gladiators were waiting, and acquitted themselves well, but it was a tough contest.

JAZZ

This highly competitive Gladiator was first bitten by the athletics bug while still in high school where she threw discus, later progressing to national level while earning a Bachelors Degree in petroleum technology. She now uses her degree in her job as a chemical lab technician at an oil and gas company in Houston, Texas. A professional bodybuilder, she has won overall awards in the Sun Belt, Houston Cup and Texas Cup competitions.

Birthplace: Lexington, Kentucky, USA
Height: 5'10"
Weight: 175lbs
Chest: 38"
Waist: 29"
Favourite Event: Duel

DYNAMITE

He may not be as tall as some of the Gladiatorial man mountains, but inch for inch Dynamite is one of the most powerful Gladiators you are ever likely to see. His incredible strength and muscle concentration make raw power his main weapon and he makes full use of it in the arena.

A professional athlete, Dynamite holds a Master in Sport from the Soviet Council on Athletics in Free-Style Wrestling and was a Champion of the Soviet Union.

His hobbies are wood sculpture and financial accounting - the first he says is to ease nerves, the second for surviving in modern Russia's harsh economic climate. He dreams one day owning his own apartment.

Born: 28th September 1963
Birthplace: Moscow, Russia
Height: 5'10"   **Weight:** 250lbs
Chest: 53"   **Bicep:** 21"
Likes: Bananas, Tchaikovsky, big guns
Favourite Event: Powerball
Favourite Phrase: "Never surrender!"

GLADIATORS 32

NOST

e very best contenders from Finland, Russia, America and the UK sweated
d strained for the title of International Champion and although there could
ly be one male and one female winner, all the contenders ably
emonstrated that they were the cream of the crop.

ICE

A standout athlete all her life, Ice played volleyball, softball and basketball in high school and won many awards. She became interested in bodybuilding and modelling after leaving school and never looked back. She has made numerous television and cinema appearances and hopes to continue with this aspect of her career in the future. Among her hobbies she lists horseback riding, martial arts and jet skiing.

Birthplace: California, USA
Height: 5'7"
Weight: 148lbs
Chest: 39"
Waist: 28"
Favourite Event: Powerball

SPARTAK

tak's family has a prestigious history. His great, great grandfather was the personal guard to Catherine the Great and his father was a champion Soviet boxer in the 200lb over division. This professional athlete holds the title of Moscow Champion and third in Soviet Union in professional armwrestling. He has also appeared in several films in his e Russia.
spite making a living by brawn, Spartak is no slouch in the brains department, having ed at the Moscow Institute of Physical Culture and Institute of Economics.

Born: 14th October 1962
Birthplace: Moscow, Russia
Height: 6'7"
Weight: 265lbs
Chest: 55"
Bicep: 21"
Likes: Listening to Bach, reading Russian poetry, Pepsi Light
Dislikes: Vodka
Favourite Event: Hit & Run
Favourite Phrase: "Victory - at all costs!"

SABRE

This tough Gladiator was a member of the notorious Bloods gang during his school years in Los Angeles and feels that his status as a Gladiator makes him a positive role model for kids in his local community, where he still lives. A successful football player before he became a Gladiator, he played for the Los Angeles Rams, the LA Raiders and the San Diego Chargers. He has made several TV appearances but uses much of his free time to speak at LA schools as a member of the Constitutional Rights Foundation. This mighty competitor can bench press 550lbs and holds a black belt in karate.

Birthplace: Nebraska, USA
Height: 6'2"
Weight: 230lbs
Chest: 52"
Bicep: 18"
Favourite Event: Powerball

HAWK

Hawk had already had a successful sporting career before he became a Gladiator. Following a distinguished football tenure in college he went on to play briefly for the Miami Dolphins in 1988. He then worked as project manager for a sports marketing company which published sports magazines throughout the United States and is currently working towards a PhD in economics and business management. He also has a burgeoning film career, having appeared in The Last Action Hero with Arnold Schwarzenegger.

Birthplace: Louisville, Kentucky, USA
Height: 6'4"
Weight: 255lbs
Chest: 48"
Bicep: 17.5"
Favourite Event: Powerball

SKY

This statuesque Gladiator was a model at the age of 12 and continues to do commercial modelling when she is not taking part in bodybuilding competitions. Never one to back away from a challenge, this mother of two goes out of her way to get involved in sports where her height is a disadvantage. In bodybuilding, for instance, she is one of the tallest and heaviest women to compete in the sport.

Birthplace: San Franciso, California, USA
Height: 6'3"
Weight: 175lbs
Chest: 39"
Waist: 30"
Favourite Event: The Wall

FLASH

Flash has a reputation in her native Finland for never say die. Even when the odds are against her she insists on striving for victory at all costs and never gives up. She works as a gym instructor while studying marketing in her homeland and seeks to inspire the same winning attitude in her students.

She lists her interests as jogging, cross country skiing and baseball, in which she has won three major Finnish titles. In Finland her Gladiator name is Salama.

Birthplace: Reisjarvi, Finland
Height: 5'6"
Weight: 154lbs
Chest: 40"
Waist: 28"
Favourite Event: Powerball

TERMINATOR

cool customer is a champion cross country skier in his own country and has over 150 awards and trophies at junior national level. He is also a keen weight r, starting at the unusually young age of 11 and continuing to this day. though a native of Finland, he has now moved to California and speaks fluent ish. His philosphy on life is to maintain a positive outlook and advises that ever bad things may look, there is always hope if you are prepared to try.

Birthplace: Hyvinkaa, Finland
Height: 6'1"
Weight: 233lbs
Chest: 50"
Bicep: 20"
Favourite Event: Hang Tough

NITRO

The most outspoken and characterful American Gladiator, Nitro was in the original Gladiator team which first hit the TV screens back in 1989. Another American football player, he was a standout linebacker at San Jose State University and has also distinguished himself as a martial arts expert. He has appeared both in films and on television and lives in Los Angeles with his son.

Birthplace: Zoma, Japan
Height: 6'2"
Weight: 218lbs
Chest: 45"
Bicep: 17"
Favourite Event: The Wall

IN PROFILE...

Don't get in the way of the charging

RHINO

DID YOU KNOW?
Rhino used to be a bodyguard and looked out for such luminaries as American presidential candidate Jesse Jackson and Britain's favourite heavyweight Frank Bruno.

Rhino may be one of the new Gladiators, but he's had the name for about as long as he can remember.

"That's my nickname. I think I got it because of the way I tra people tell me it's because of the noises I make, but I've nev heard a rhino train so I couldn't say."

"I was over the moon when I was picked to be a Gladiator. When I tried out for the programme they made me climb a rope, do some speed running and some general exercises. T was only one guy who could keep up with me and he turned out to be Raider!

"I've had to adapt my training programme since I became a Gladiator. Before, I did mostly body building, but now I'm do more aerobic stuff - step aerobics, Stairmaster, treadmill, tha kind of thing. I find I'm having to watch my diet now as well which I didn't used to do."

Rhino has proved himself to be a bit of an all-rounder on the Ultimate Challenge, and is hard pressed to pick a favourite.

"I like Gauntlet, Atlaspheres, Joust, Duel - a bit of everything really."

One thing contenders could have learned from David Attenborough: it doesn't pay to get in the way of a charging Rhino.

STATISTICS
Date of Birth: 30th September 1969
Home: West London
Height: 5' 11"
Weight: 18 stone
Chest: 54"
Waist: 32"
Bicep: 20"

GLADIATORS 37

IN PROFILE...

Aiming to get stuck in a lot more from now on!

COBRA

DID YOU KNOW?
Cobra went white water rafting in Africa with Hunter this year and their Gladiators' training came in very handy when they were chased by an irate bull elephant!

Cobra found a good way to combine work with pleasu[re] when, prior to the live Gladiators show at Sheffield la[st] Easter, he decided to step up his training in the glorious sunshine of Hawaii!

"I'm smitten with the place!" he exclaims. "I went whale-spotting on a catamaran - well, if they weren't whales, they were very big guppies! - and I got a nice tan. They've got a 47,000 sq. ft. Gold's gym there, with everything that you nee[d] and it's really relaxing.

"When I'm preparing for Gladiators, I don't want to be under any tension. Some of the lads and lassies went to Lanzarote where the Olympic athletes and boxers train, but training wi[th] everyone else would make me tense. This way, I could do m[y] weight training and then lie on the beach and chill out. And [it] worked, because I did really well at Sheffield."

His schedule has been so tight that Cobra had to make do w[ith] training in the UK before filming the new series, but he's sti[ll] been putting in plenty of hard work, working out at least five days a week. "I've just bought an expensive bicycle, because [I] love my cycling, especially when the weather's nice," he comments.

During the last series, he suffered from a number of injuries, but this time, but now he's back in peak physical condition. [I] want to get a lot more stuck in from now on!" he promises. Watch out, contenders!

GLADIATORS 38

STATISTICS

Date of Birth: 29th October 1963
Home: Belvedere, Kent
Height: 6'
Weight: 14 stone 7 lbs
Chest: 48"
Waist: 30"
Bicep: 18"

IN PROFILE...

NIGHTSHADE
The deadly, formidable opponent

Six foot Nighshade is always a formidable opponent - but she's even more deadly now than when she first started! This year, she has stepped her training schedule up to a minimum of three hours work a day.

"I like any sort of exercise that is done to music - aerobic exercise, step exercise and things like that," she says. "With introduction of Pyramid, I've taken to stair running - and by I mean real stairs! I find a really high building or a car park and go up and down their stairs, very early in the morning when really quiet, if they'll let me! I wanted to do that, because I wanted to make sure that I was as specifically fit as possible because the contenders have got so good. I know that I'm in absolutely top shape when I can get to the top of a hotel in a number of seconds!

"So I don't always go to a gym to train. In fact, I've got a very simple circuit that I do that I call 'maintenance' and I can do that anywhere, even in a hotel room. It consists of press-ups, back extensions, sit-ups and squats, and you can do that in ten minutes."

However, it's not only brawn that makes a successful Gladiator and Nightshade knows that mental agility is equally important when taking part in the Ultimate Challenge.

"The contenders are getting smarter, too," she reports. "They been watching the events and they're developing their own tactics and strategies for winning them. So we just have to get smarter too!"

DID YOU KNOW?
Nightshade loves to listen to music on her Walkman to motivate her before she steps into the arena and the track she most likes to hear before she takes part in Duel is Grace Jones' Demolition Man!

STATISTICS

Date of Birth: 14th November 1960
Home: Birmingham
Height: 6'
Weight: 11 stone
Chest: 36"
Waist: 27"

GLADIATORS 41

IN PROFILE...

WARRIOR
...Not a man of routine

For the largest of all the Gladiators, variety is the spice of life, because Warrior likes to alter his exercise routine from day to day, in order to keep himself motivated.

"I'm not a man of routine," he explains. "I have to change it around and very rarely do the same thing twice. Diversifying the time keeps your enthusiasm high, because it *is* hard work.

"A couple of years ago, my training was nearly always just gym work, lifting weights and trying to put on body mass, but now I've got to be a combination of a boxer, an athlete and a body builder. I'm trying to keep my weight up and still keep really because I've got to run around and do events like the Pyramid which really suits a smaller guy, so I do lots of running on the beach, step-ups and aerobics, alongside my heavy weightlifting. That way, I can get cardiovascularly fit, as well as keeping the look. And I work out with the Tranmere Rovers team now and again, and those guys get you pretty fit!"

Even when he has some time off, Warrior still likes to be involved in sport; his main hobby is golf, which he loves to play whenever he can. "It's a great game, and it means I can get in the fresh air and away from all the weight-training and weightlifting," he enthuses. "I used play off a three handicap, but I'm playing off around eight at the moment, and I'd like to get as good as I can. I play a lot of charity pro-amateur and celebrity-amateur events around the country and I've won quite a few, so I'm going to try to get more silver and crystalware on the mantelpiece this year!"

DID YOU KNOW?

Warrior really is an all-round athlete; as well being a former body building champion before he joined Gladiators, he was also a ranked decathlete.

GLADIATORS 42

STATISTICS

Date of Birth: 30th December 1960
Home: Wirral, Merseyside
Height: 6' 5"
Weight: 19 stone 8 lbs
Chest: 55"
Waist: 38"
Bicep: 22"

GLADIATORS 43

IN PROFILE...

The former European and UK Aerobic Champion

VOGUE

This former European and UK Aerobic Champion made her Gladiatorial debut at the Gladiators' live shows staged at Sheffield last Easter. Although she had already passed an audition to take part in the show, she says her live performance was crucial in determining whether she would become a permanent team member - but she passed the Ultimate Challenge with flying colours!

"It's all very well being fit," she observes, "but if you can't actually perform in front of a crowd and complete the events you're no good to the Gladiators! I think I proved myself at Sheffield and I haven't looked back since!"

From the live shows, she's already picked out two events that she thinks may become favourites in future. "I liked the Pyramid," she says. "I've had a gymnastic background, so the tumbling and falling didn't scare me, whereas it might frighten other people, and I'm quite fast, so climbing up and down was good fun. And I liked Atlaspheres as well."

Vogue found her early taster at the live shows to be of invaluable help when it came to the real thing in front of the cameras for the series. "Until I went to Sheffield, I'd never seen a live show before, I'd only seen it on the telly," she comments, "but it is a completely different experience, seeing it live. I think that experience helped me to be a bit better prepared mentally for the new series."

DID YOU KNOW?

Fot the last three years Vogue has been a member of the team that won the National Aerobic Championship and also became European champions two years ago.

GLADIATORS 44

STATISTICS

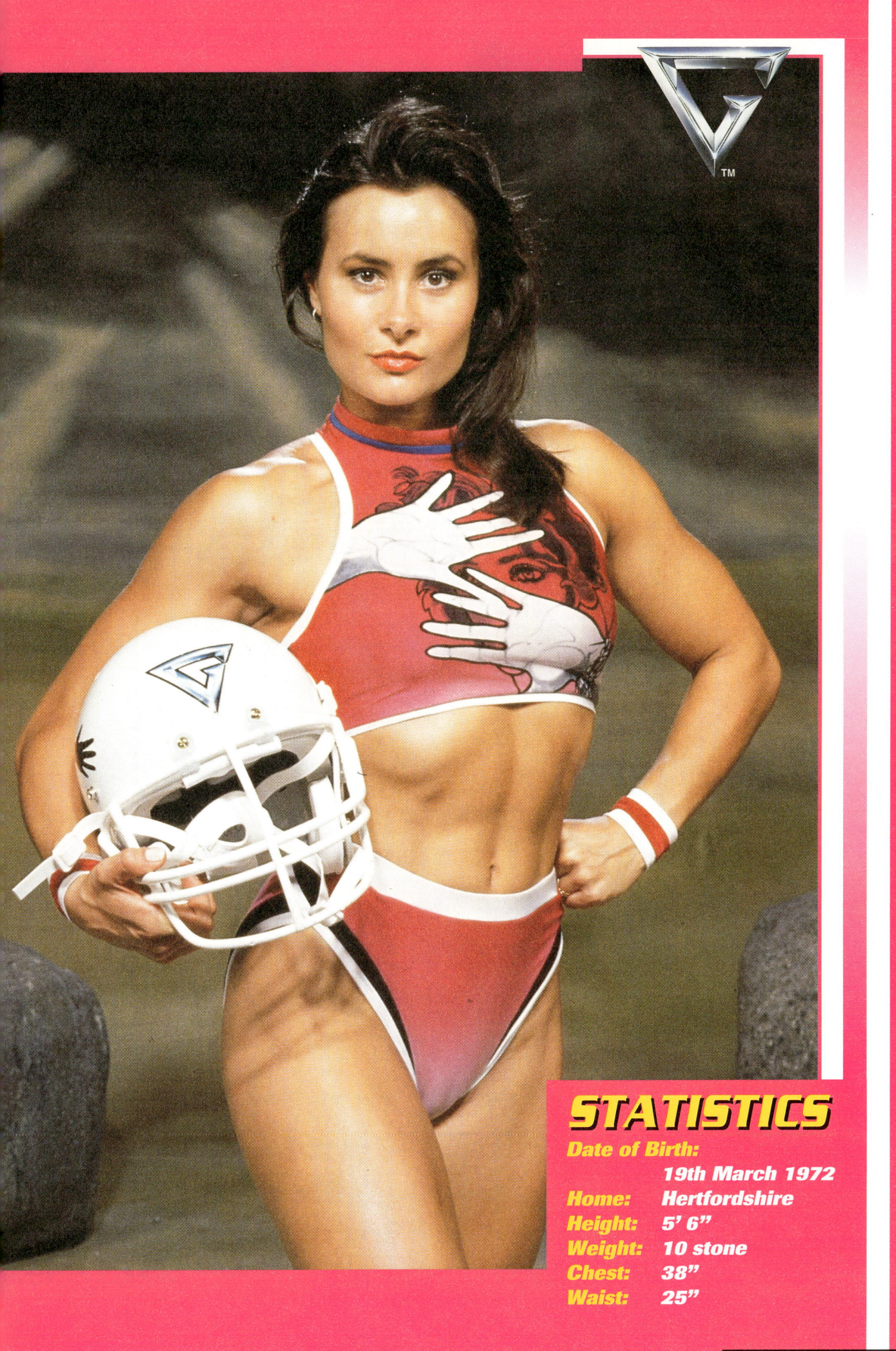

Date of Birth:
19th March 1972
Home: Hertfordshire
Height: 5' 6"
Weight: 10 stone
Chest: 38"
Waist: 25"

GLADIATORS 45

COBRA

How long did you study martial arts for before you became an expert?
Martin Hillier (14), Brighton.

Cobra says: "You never become an expert in martial arts - you can always learn more. I started a bit of judo and boxing when I was seven or eight, so it's been about 22 years. I've got lots of mates who are champions at this and that, so I still talk to and muck about with them."

TROJAN

When is your birthday?
Louise Austin, London.

Trojan says: "25th February, which makes me a Pisces. I've been told that I'm a typical Pisces - a bit of a dreamer, imaginative, ambitious - and useless with money!"

ZODIAC

I know that you're an athlete all the time, even when you're taking part in Gladiators. What sort of diet do you have to ma sure you stay fit and healthy?
Helen Trice (12), Reading.

Zodiac says: "I try not to get too obsessed about my di When you are at the very top of your sport, it's important watch what you eat, because you're trying to get the la one per cent added to your performance, so I eat everythi that will give me as much energy as possible. But really, y should just try to eat a very balanced diet, and that's wh I do. When you are doing exercise, you are burning up much, it doesn't really matter if you occasionally e chocolate!"

FALCON

Why do you like the Wall best? Which event is the most popular?
Alice Keeling, Cheshire.

Falcon says: "I used to like the Wall best, but now I must admit, I prefer Pyramid or Pursuit. Pyramid is a good physical event and it looks quite spectacular on screen. Pursuit is like a mini-Eliminator or the kind of obstacle race you did at school, and I always used to like them!"

YOUR QUESTIONS ANSWERED

Readers of Gladiators Magazine had plenty to ask the Gladiators about themselves and the show. Here is a selection of questions which didn't make it into the magazine.

NIGHTSHADE

I love the dance you do when you beat someone at Duel. Have you ever done any dancing training and what kind of music do you like?
Kelly Henry (12), London.

Nightshade says: "I haven't done any dance training, but I do like dance music, chart music and soulful music. I have a huge collection of records that stretches from classical to jazz to choral, so I really do love music and use it very much to motivate me to play games, help me with relaxation and all sorts of things, not just for dancing."

PANTHER

Hi! I am a big fan of the Gladiators. My favourite Gladiator is Panther, but are any of the Gladiators keen swimmers? I am, I have won a silver medal in synchronised swimming.
Joanna Liza Wilson (11), Attleborough, Norfolk.

Panther says: "I don't know about the other Gladiators, but I never used to be very keen on swimming, because I didn't like getting my eyes wet! However, I have overcome that and quite like swimming now. In fact, I'd like to have a go at scuba diving!"

WOLF

Are you really as bad as you pretend to be?
Damon Wallace, Liverpool.

Wolf says: "Absolutely! 110 per cent!"

LIGHTNING

I am 14 years old and I have three little brothers called Brian, Colin and Paul. We all watch Gladiators every week and see you doing all different kinds of tumbles. I wish I was able to do them, but I have tried and have been unable to do them. Can you tell me how you are able to do all different kinds of tumbles?
Marie Paterson, Glasgow.

Lightning says: "My ten years' experience as a gymnast means that I am strong and supple enough to do those tumbles. However, if you want to try them yourself, you should make sure you warm up first and get good coaching. You should definitely not try to do them unaided and without expert help, or you could hurt yourself."

HUNTER

You always seem to be smiling and having a good time in Gladiators, but do you ever get angry with any of the contenders?
Christine Magee (14), Norwich.

Hunter says: "If I've performed as well as I can and the contender has as well and has beaten me, that's fair enough. But when, for example, I remember once I slipped a couple of times on the Wall, which lost me a second and the contender got past me - then I got annoyed with myself. But I never get angry with a contender."

JET

Would you please tell me your favourite film and who your favourite actor and actress are?
Brodie Field, Telford.

Jet says: "My favourite actresses are Jodie Foster and Kathy Bates; I would make an effort to go and see them, whatever film they're in. Actorwise, I do like Gerard Depardieu, and Dan Day Lewis is absolutely brilliant!"

WARRIOR

Was it very hard trying to get up the Wall because you are so big and heavy?
Samantha Braine (9), Tyneside.

Warrior says: "It is difficult, because it's not a big man's game. I had to prove a lot of people wrong last year, because they goaded me that I couldn't do the Wall, but that's why I'm a Gladiator, because I take up challenges and try to overcome them. So I got stuck in, practised it and did well."

SARACEN

I love watching you swinging from ring to ring in Hang Tough and you make it look so easy. I think you're really good at all the events you do. I want to take up bodybuilding but my mum says I'm too young. when is a good time to start?
James McBride (11), Nottingham.

Saracen says: "When you're growing, weight training can be detrimental to you and can actually stunt your growth, so I'd wait until you were in your late teens before you start training with weights. However, gymnastics is very good for building up strength and stamina and I wish I'd taken it up when I was younger, because it is a very good body conditioner. You can start gymnastics from four or five years old and there are plenty of good gymnastics clubs around the country."

COMPETITION WINNERS

The winner!

Toby Black (5), Beddington, Surrey.

"If I could become a Gladiator, the name I would choose would be Fox.

"I would choose this name because my favourite Gladiator is Wolf."

Thank you, Toby, there's a smashing bicycle from Cycleurope UK on its way to you.

We had a tremendous response to last year's competition and it's taken us literally days to wade through the letters we received. Thanks to everyone for entering, but unfortunately we could only have one outright winner.

The question you had to answer was "Which Gladiator didn't begin body-building until he was 19?"

The answer was, of course, Saracen.

We also asked you to suggest a name for yourself if you were to become a Gladiator. You all did very well, and some of them may even be considered as names for real-life Gladiators in the future.

The Runners-up!

The three runners-up will all receive a selection of Gladiators games from Paul Lamond Games.

Douglas Couttie (10), Glasgow.

"If I could become a Gladiator, the name I would choose would be T-Rex.

"I would choose this name because it sounds mighty and mean."

Rebecca Stewart (7), Bacup, Lancashire.

"If I could become a Gladiator, the name I would choose would be Star.

"I would choose this name because I look bright."

Gordon MacFarlane (5), Dunfermline.

"If I could become a Gladiator, the name I would choose would be Jewel.

"I would choose this name because a jewel shines."

nd here is a selection
f some of the best
ames, which
nfortunately couldn't
in, but they're all
orth printing.

edator
ecause I would claim a lot of
tims."
rtin Clough (9),
erseyside.

sh
ecause I can run fast."
ul Gilbert (11),
effield.

er
ecause it's my favourite word."
rc Webb (7),
ading, Berks.

mstone
ecause I'd be strong and
autiful."
cinda Hall (7),
rrey.

ider
ecause I can run fast like a
der."
roline Turner (8),
lingham, Kent.

under
ecause I would be the biggest
se in the arena."
omas Cornell (9),
dford.

o:
ecause like the thunder in a
storm, I too have a strong and
determined character."
Abigail Turner (11),
Gillingham, Kent.

Nightjet
"Because I like Nightshade and Jet."
Kayleigh Palmer(9),
Great Yarmouth.

Planet
"Because I would be the biggest and best Gladiator on this planet."
Nicholas Williams (10),
Welling, Kent.

T-Bone
"Because I am tough and beefy."
Tom Evans (6),
Market Drayton, Shropshire.

Hercules
"Because I want to grow up big and strong."
David Smith (7),
Manchester.

Bulldog
"Because it's British, strong and a winner."
Michael Lowther,
London.

Terror
"Because I can really terrorise my opponents."
Robert Liszczyk (14),
Leicester.

Cheetah
"Because they're fast and furious."
Jilly Llewellyn (10),
Cheltenham.

Diamond
"Because it sparkles and it does not break."
Gemma Carter (8),
Welwyn Garden City.

Sphinx
"Because with the head of a woman, I would have the strength of a lioness."
Sarah Tiller (9),
Epsom Downs, Surrey.

Terminator
"Because I would terminate the contenders."
Antonio Dichello (5),
Worthing, Sussex.

Figaro
"Because I'm little and cute."
Alexandra Holmes (2),
Liverpool.

Speed
"Because I would go so fast on all the events."
John Potts (10),
Stoke-On-Trent.

Snake
"Because I'm thin, tall and wild."
Rachel Daykin (11),
West Midlands.

Destroyer
"Because I fight a lot."
Ricky Williams(9),
Chatham, Kent.

IN PROFILE...

Ready for the Challenge!
PANTHER

Gladiators fans were pleased to see for themselves that after suffering a horrific accident, injuring her lower back when she fell awkwardly off Tilt in the 1995 series, Panther is now fully restored to fitness and taking part in the Ultimate Challenge once again!

However, she needed all her courage and determination to fight her way back to health and admits that at one time, when she was undergoing a five month period of physiotherapy that kept her out of the gym, she wondered if she would ever be able to compete as a Gladiator again. However, once she started training again in February, she slowly built her strength up until she was fit enough to successfully compete in the live shows last Easter. Since then, there's been no stopping her!

"Whereas before, because I'm from a body-building background, I did more weight training, and cycling and running for distance rather than speed, I've changed that now and I do short, sharp bursts of training. I do shuttle runs and run around with big weights to get my speed up, and it helps muscle growth as well. I've also taken up boxing training and that's helped me with the power for the Duel - and apparently, I have a very strong uppercut! And I've just enlisted a chap who will help me with some rugby tackling!"

Now that Panther is back in the arena, she's fitter than ever and raring to go!

"I think because I injured myself so badly and was at such a low ebb, it made me realise life really is worth living," she enthuses. "You should live it to the full and I am really enjoying everything now. I'm ready for the challenge!"

DID YOU KNOW?
Panther has two pet iguanas and because they have such enormous appetites, she calls them Warrior and Hunter!

STATISTICS

Date of Birth:
    14th October 1963
Home: Slough
Height: 5' 7"
Weight: 9 stone 10 lb
Chest: 36"
Waist: 24"

GLADIATORS 51

IN PROFILE...

RAIDER

"The Raider's business is to attack and that's what I do!"

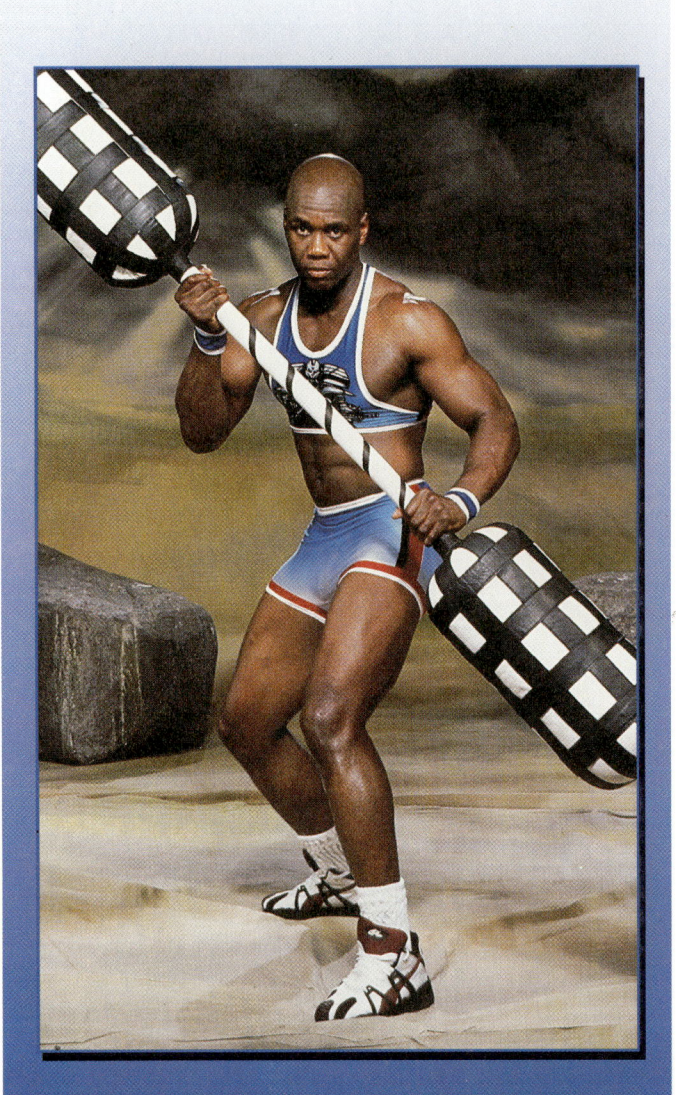

Raider is one Gladiator who feels his name suits his personality perfectly.

"A raider's business is to attack, and that's what I do. I'm relentless when I want to win, I don't let up."

This former physical education teacher is no stranger to competition - he's been a practising martial arts expert for o[ver] 13 years.

"I practise the Korean art of Tae Kwon Do. It's one of the old[est] forms of martial art and is mostly about kicking - about 85 p[er] cent. That helps me with speed, stamina and all-round fitnes[s.] I've got my first dan and hopefully soon I'll be going for my second.

"I'm also doing more weights now to try to build myself up. Saying that, though, you don't really need to be all that big, [the] main thing is to be powerful, and to have a lot of stamina. When the contenders come on, the Gladiators should be in control - they're stepping into our office so we need to be ab[le] to go the full distance."

There is at least one big difference between Raider and the [rest] of the Gladiators - he likes Joust!

"A lot of them say they don't like that event but I love it! You[´re] up there in the middle of nowhere, balancing on your sky bik[e,] brandishing a big club, beating the living daylights out of the other guy. It's good. I want to make that event my own."

DID YOU KNOW?
Raider is an artist and likes nothing better than to draw sketches in his spare time.

GLADIATORS 52

STATISTICS

Date of Birth:
	17th September 1963
Home:	South London
Height:	6'3"
Weight:	16 stone, 6lbs
Chest:	46"
Waist:	29"
Bicep:	18"

GLADIATORS 53

IN PROFILE...

FALCON
Pouncing on contenders like a bird of prey

Watching this Gladiator pouncing on contenders like her namesake bird of prey, it's hard to believe that she suffers from nerves before every event! "But as soon as game starts, my nerves just go, because you have to get on with the performance," she says.

Falcon is well aware that, as with most sports, mental attitude is at least as important to success in the Gladiators events as strength and fitness. "If you're not psyched out mentally, those contenders can run circles around you!" she laughs. "I've learnt that myself, because although I had the strength and fitness, the first series I felt I lacked the psych. Now, I take time to mentally prepare myself.

"Last year, before an event, I would find a space of my own take a few minutes by myself, to deep breathe and think ahead about the event that I am about to do and all the different ways that I can tackle the person, looking at it in my mind and preparing a mental picture before I go out."

But despite the physical and mental demands the show makes on the Gladiators, Falcon wouldn't want to be doing anything else! "It's great when I'm in Tesco and children come up and say, 'Hello, Falcon - you're my favourite Gladiator!'" she enthuses. "It's nice to be a role model for the youngsters and think you are helping them, by bringing fitness to the forefront in their lives at a young age."

DID YOU KNOW?
Falcon's favourite actor is Arnold Schwarzenegger and she has seen all of his films!

GLADIATORS 54

STATISTICS

Date of Birth: 6th November 1963
Home: Basingstoke, Hants
Height: 5' 7"
Weight: 10 and a half stone
Chest: 38"
Waist: 25"

GLADIATORS 55

John & Ulrika's MAGIC MOMENTS

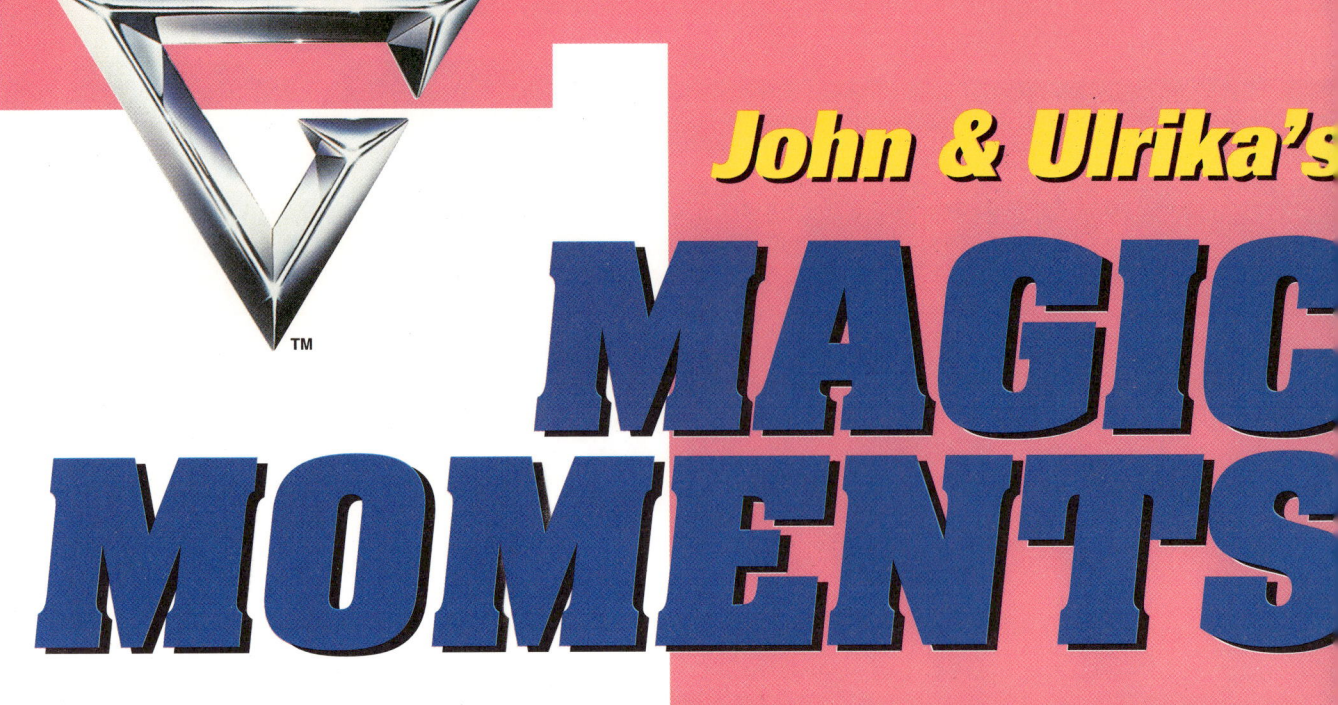

Gladiators presenters John Fashanu and Ulrika Jonsson remember some personal highlights from the last series...

JOHN FASHANU

"One of the highlights of the last series for me was Two Sco[tt], the contender from America, on the International Gladiators. [He] was a majestic character, the ultimate Gladiator - even thou[gh] he was a contender! He was fit, he was very quick, he was [very] humorous - he really was a fantastic contender! I've never s[een] an athlete like him.

"Also, I did enjoy seeing how powerful Nightshade was in th[e] last series. She really is in a class of her own. You can see s[he's] got the discipline of being an individual in athletics, as oppo[sed] to team games; she was the lady Daley Thompson and it rea[lly] tells. She doesn't want to lose and she doesn't mind getting hurt. She'll give knocks, but she'll also take them.

"The introduction of International Gladiators can only show w[ho] is the best in the world. This thing is really getting universal [and] everybody's talking about it! I called up one of my friends in Tanzania and they were watching it over there, because the[y] bought the video cassettes in London! So that shows you wh[at's] happening and how it's really taking off.

"This is my fourth year of presenting the Gladiators and I lo[ok] forward to every series. It's grown larger, bigger and better, [and] the Gladiators are getting stronger all the time. Gladiators is going from strength to strength to strength!"

ULRIKA JONSSON

[Wh]en we started the last series, I was six months pregnant [and] when we finished, I was seven and a half months pregnant, [fo]r me, it was not just the challenge of doing another series [and] meeting lots of new contenders and new games, but doing [it wi]th another little person inside me! Everybody was always [getti]ng me chairs and getting me glasses of water, and all the [gladi]ators kept coming along and patting me on the tummy, so [ever]ybody looked after me really well, and I felt very special!

"Once again, new games like Pyramid and Poleaxe were really, really exciting. Every year the contenders get stronger and stronger, but you also meet nicer and nicer people every time - particularly Eunice (Huthart, overall women's champion in 1995). From the moment I met her, I thought, 'Here's a winner!', and as she began to win the heats, I thought, 'Yes, she's definitely going to win the whole thing.' She nearly let me down, when she almost lost it on the Travelator, and it was so exciting! Everyone kept saying, 'Ulrika, calm down!' But when you're watching the events, you don't feel as if you're working and it almost becomes a bonus to get wrapped up in all the excitement. It's really good fun and you never get fed up with it. I've done four series and I still thoroughly enjoy doing it.

"I wish I had been part of the International Gladiators last year, but physically, that was quite impossible. The latest series has been a lot more work for me this time, but that's the whole essence of the Gladiators - providing people with a challenge - and this has been mine!"

THE WINNER

Winners aren't born, they're made, and last year's Gladiators champs dedicated eve...

EUNICE – CAN'T MISS!

Eunice Huthart kept her good humour, down-to-earth attitude and fighting spirit throughout the tough heats to reach and win the final of Gladiators. And she couldn't have been happier!

Not bad going for a woman who hadn't even planned to enter the competition.

She explains: "My friends and family kept telling me that I should enter. Because of the sport I'm involved in, I have to have all-round physical strength and stamina.

"A few people applied for me to enter Gladiators and before I knew it, four application forms had landed through my letterbox.

"I didn't think I'd do anything, but when we went to the try-outs, the bug bit me. It gave me a good indication of my fitness levels compared to others."

Eunice is no stranger to testing her fitness - at the time of entering she was the British and European kickboxing champion and ranked number three in the world.

She won £5,000 prize-money for taking on the Gladiators and proving she was the best contender in the series. She spent some of the cash on a dream holiday to Greece for herself and her family, but she sold the jeep and used the money as the deposit on a new home.

What's her advice to contenders who hope to be as successful as her in upcoming shows?

"It's not so much the physical ability that gets you through, it's the mental attitude. Once you get that right, you will go a lot further."

All contenders admit they have at least one favourite event. The Gauntlet proved to be Eunice's favourite, "because of the contact and power involved".

While all the Gladiators do their best to help out the contenders, Eunice claims she received most support from Jet.

"Jet always seemed to have time for everyone," she says. "She was really friendly and was always there for advice."

Jet's advice certainly paid off for this winner, who shows no sign of slowing down!

STATISTICS

AGE: ....
HEIGHT: 5ft 7
WEIGHT: .... .10 sto
HOME: .... .Liverpo

...ounce of commitment and ability to success in the Ultimate Challenge.

PAUL – AHEAD OF THE FIELD

STATISTICS

AGE: 28
HEIGHT: 6ft
WEIGHT ....14 stone
HOME: ....South Oxhey

Super-policeman Paul Field took a break from walking the beat to stomping the competition when he took on the might of the Gladiators to swing to victory in the finals.

Paul, an Olympic bobsleigher and decathlete, is used to competing, but admits he found Gladiators a bit of a strain.

"I really enjoyed it," he says, "but it was stressful. Being in the Olympics before and being an international athlete, everyone reckoned it would be easy for me and there was a lot of pressure from friends and family."

He plans to take his wife Natalie and their three children, eight-year-old Dan, six-year-old Adam and six month-old Jack on holiday to Disneyland with his £5,000 win.

Jack was born in the middle of the Gladiators series, between the heats and the quarter final - which meant Paul didn't get any training in between those rounds!

"It was really hectic," admitted Paul. "Natalie was in hospital for five days and I was rushing between the boys at home and the hospital. After Jack was born, it was difficult for me to get motivated again. I wanted to be at home with Natalie and the baby.

"It was Natalie who finally got me going again, I'd almost lost interest, but she told me to get my finger out and get myself back up to Birmingham for the quarter-finals."

While it's always great to have the support of friends and family while taking part in Gladiators, Paul advised future contenders that it's most important to believe in yourself.

"If you don't believe in yourself, you're never going to achieve," says Paul. "Don't set your aims too high, be realistic. Once you achieve those aims, then set slightly higher ones. Never be satisfied."

Good advice for anyone who plans to tackle the fearsome Gladiators in the next series.
However, one Gladiator who didn't strike fear into Paul's heart was Wolf - the man everyone loves to hate. Paul shatters Wolf's hard-man image by saying: "He's a really nice guy and a very good actor. If you ask anyone on the street who their favourite Gladiator is, 50 per cent will say Wolf. He's got a very big following."

Hang Tough proved to be Paul's best, and favourite, event during the contest. None of the Gladiators he came up against on the aerial ring game managed to pull him down and he won 10 points each time he took part.

"You need a lot of upper body strength and agility to take part in Hang Tough. Being a decathlete, I have to do the high jump, long jump and pole vaulting, so that keeps me pretty agile."

Paul's next challenge should be at the 1996 Olympic Games when he hopes to compete in athletics.

GLADIATORS 59

GLADIATORS COMPETITION

Don't miss your chance to win one of these terrific bikes from Cycleurope UK in our great easy-to-enter competition!

All you have to do is answer this simple question, the answer to which you can find elsewhere in this book:

Which Gladiator claims their pet dog is their best training partner?

... and then tell us which is your favourite event and why.

Complete the entry form on the next page and send it to the address shown, to arrive before Monday 1st February 1996.

Send a photocopy if you don't want to cut the page.

The reader sending the first correct entry drawn on 1st February 1996 will win a boy's or girl's bicycle from Cycleurope UK, matched to the winner's age.

The next ten entries drawn will receive either a selection of Gladiators games from Hornby Games or a smashing Wolf T-shirt from Nutmeg Mills (size: extra large, one size fits all).

Gladiators bicycle suitable for younger children

1ST PRIZE

Gladiators bicycle suitable for older children (similar to one shown)

RUNNERS-UP PRIZES

ENTRY FORM

Question: Which Gladiator claims their pet dog is their best training partner?

Answer: ....

My favourite event is: ....

Because: ....

Your name: ....

Age: ....

Your height (to determine frame size of bicycle): ....

Address: ....

.... Postcode: ....

Send your entry to:
Gladiators Competition, Marketing Department,
Egmont Publishing Ltd, PO Box 111, Great Ducie Street, Manchester M60 3BL

RULES

Employees of World International or their respective agents may not enter this competition.

The editor's decision is final and no correspondence will be entered into.

A list of winners' names will be available on request and on receipt of a SAE after 14th February 1996. The publishers reserve the right to vary the prizes, subject to availability at the time of judging the competition.

GLADIATORS 61